MW01173328

EVERYTHING IS PERSONAL

Embracing Stewardship in the Workplace and Everyplace

LOUIS RODEN

Defining Moments Press

Defining Moments Press, Inc.

For more information, visit https://inspirelsc.com.

Cover Design: 99designs

Editing: Kat Spencer

DEDICATION

This book is dedicated to my family. Not an unusual dedication, I know. But without them, who would push us? Challenge us? Delight us? Frustrate us while we frustrate them? It is all such beautiful madness...

To my parents:

Richard 'Dick' Roden—I miss you, Dad. You taught me that a kind word is always a better choice than a harsh one.

Elizabeth 'Betty' Roden—Your belief in me brings me strength to this day. I love you, Momma.

Deep thanks to my sons, Joon Ho and Tae Ho. They have been my muse in so many ways and have helped me learn what it takes to be a leader and a father, whether they intended to or not!

And deep from within my heart, thank you to my wife, companion, and partner Soledad—without her encouragement, love, and support, I would be lost.

TABLE OF CONTENTS

FOREWORD

By Tae Ho Roden

Honestly, I used to think my dad was a spy. No joke.

He would head off in a suit, and say he was going to China, or Thailand, or Germany, or Brazil, or some other mysterious place to a kid like me. I asked him why, and he always said the same thing. "I'm going to do leadership training, Bud!" Sure, Dad. You're a spy.

And he always brought back such cool toys and gifts!

Finally, after culinary school, he brought me along. First locally, then internationally. I not only started to see what he did firsthand, I got to do it with him. I love culinary, don't get me wrong; it will always be a part of who I am and what I do. But hospitality in general, and leadership specifically, felt like home—because it *was* home.

Now I understood. The things that we talk about in these training classes were echoed at home when we were growing up. Be kind. Demonstrate respect. Build trust through everything that you do. And remember, most of all, that every decision you make has a consequence, and that consequence is yours to own.

And it was refreshing to know my dad wasn't a spy.

ACKNOWLEDGEMENTS

To the leaders I have had the pleasure to work with in and out of the hospitality industry ... without you all, the evolution of the ideas within this book would have never taken form. There are too many wonderful colleagues to be able to note them all, but I would be remiss if I didn't share the names of the friends, colleagues, and mentors below that have mattered so much:

Tony Quinn—the first 'boss' I had that wasn't just a manager, but a leader.

John Perry—a leader who led us through the dot-com demise and into a brave new world.

Joe Terzi—my first leader at Starwood Hotels, and still one of the finest examples I can think of when I consider all a leader needs to be.

Key leaders throughout my time at Starwood, who represented engaged leadership at every turn: Geoff Ballotti, Rick Suhl, Margie Sitton, Matt Redmond, Roland Vos, and so many more.

Juan Cortes, Clark Witten, Bill O'Mara, and the entire Starwood Organizational Capability team that helped spread our leadership gospel around the world.

And all the warriors of the heart at any level, in any industry, that persevere every day to make a positive difference in the lives of others. You all reflect the true power and meaning of leadership.

INTRODUCTION

In 1897 Mark Twain wrote a book called **Following the Equator**, one of his many musings about traveling the world and the wonderous experiences that unfolded. He once handwrote a dedication in that book that I have often pondered...

"Be good, and you will be lonesome."

Like many things, Twain left the meaning of that simple line to the reader. I have come to derive my own meaning, and it has helped inspire me through bouts of self-doubt and insecurity, not to mention long trips through dark airports in so many corners of the world.

For me? Being 'good' means staying still: professionally, personally, even practically. Do what you're supposed to do. What society tells you to do, whatever society you are part of. Mine was the Midwest of the United States, my childhood being spent in northeast Ohio. Grow up, stay out of trouble, go to school, get a job, do just a little better than your parents did, get a mortgage, have kids, consume your savings and your pension in old age, and, well, say goodnight.

The lonesome part? Well, that's just doing the same thing, day in and day out. Not much new … not much scary … just sameness. Just grey. And the years slip away.

That's a different sort of loneliness.

There is nothing wrong with being happy and content in whatever you're doing. But if you never extend yourself at all, time just passes, and you just get old. You need to reach out beyond the comfortable or the usual. As the filmmaker Alejandro Jodorowsky said: "Birds born in a cage think flying is an illness."

I never thought I would look back at the instability and uncertainty in my life and see it as a gift as I do now. How many times I prayed for stability—in a particular job, relationship, or place…

Truly, unanswered prayers are often a gift.

CHAPTER ONE

Leading with Stewardship

"Leadership is not about being in charge. It's about taking care of those in your charge."

—*Simon Sinek*

It's business, it's not personal.

Every time I hear this, I sigh. This simple phrase has given people, bosses, governments, and every other person who has proclaimed it some sort of rationale in order to take the humanity out of decisions, especially difficult ones.

Why is it cringe-worthy? Because it is pure nonsense.

It's **bullshit.**

Everything is personal. Especially business. In fact, when you make difficult decisions that impact people, it is deeply personal, to the person making the decision and those impacted by it. Anyone saying different is just running for cover—leaders need to stop hiding behind the 'business' aspect. Your decisions small and large impact people. Accept it. Own it. Hell, **embrace it.**

Think about the amount of time you spend at work … in your career … doing what you do. If we don't count sleeping as 'being at home'—because we are not in a conscious state, for crying out loud—then we are spending 75–80 percent of our waking lives at work. I don't think anyone wants to spend literally most of their lives in an impersonal place! Now, that doesn't mean we take a self-centered approach to every business decision in the workplace—that's different and something that we'll consider when we discuss self-management and self-awareness a bit later—but it does, and should, significantly impact the lens of how we view our time working—that is to say, how we spend nearly 80 percent of our lives.

Leaders need to understand and accept this premise. It's a shift from the old idea of simply providing a fair day's pay for a fair day's work. That isn't enough, and has never been enough, for people. We need to change the lens if we want our teams to not only be satisfied, but truly engaged and committed in their roles and careers.

Some bosses see the agreement as only that. You work. I give you money for that work. Contract completed. That's just boring, dismissive, and not only uninspiring, but emotionally exhausting. It's just a different form of prostitution. People, whether they fully understand it or not, want more. And what they want isn't just an absence of negativity ... or the absence of risk or danger ... they desire an environment worthy of 80 percent of their lives! People will spend more time with their co-workers and leaders than they will with their children, spouse, partner, or family. Leaders need to carefully consider what they want that 80 percent to look like for their teams.

Of course, people are there to do a job. We understand that. It's no different from my job as a parent or a partner—there are expectations, and I seek to exceed those expectations at every opportunity. However, successful leaders embrace this shift of not simply accounting for 80 percent of people's lives by just trading money for it—they accept **stewardship**.

Stewardship

What do we mean by stewardship? It's a simple premise really. Think of your team members approaching you and saying "Here boss. Here is 80 percent of my life. It's in your hands on what kind of environment I will be in, how committed I will be, how hard I will work, and how creative or innovative I will be, all predicated on how you will treat me and engage me while I spend MOST of my waking life with you."

Our team members may never make that statement, but it is the truth for all of them. What will our answer be? *"Just get to work"?* That won't do—not if we want to build committed, engaged, successful teams. A place where people WANT to spend 80 percent of their lives. We must accept stewardship of that 80 percent—and that is leadership through a significantly different lens.

So, what does accepting stewardship mean for leaders? It begins by understanding the importance related to how people spend the majority of their lives—even if they often don't. Viewing the 'leader–team member' relationship through the lens of stewardship impacts how we engage them in every aspect. It's a different level of responsibility for the leader. But once we understand it, we earn team member trust, respect, high performance, and loyalty. So many organizations are looking for the magic solution to employee performance, employee retention, and even effective recruiting. **This is it.**

The Golden Rule

Let's start our examination of stewardship by exploring the Golden Rule—an idea popular in many cultures, and the hallmark of many leadership postings on social media, and even in many books.

"Treat others the way you want to be treated."

This is just wrong. It's not only wrong; it works **against** the idea of stewardship.

Why? Firstly, it is a self-centered, myopic approach. It is a bit pompous to think or assume that everyone wants to be treated the way **you** want to be treated. Only YOU want to be treated the way you want to be treated.

The key to stewardship, and inspired leadership, is to treat people the way *THEY* want to be treated. The Golden Rule, my friends, is backwards.

For example, you may love public praise and feedback. You may feel great pride and a sense of worth when your boss brings you in front of the entire team and speaks about your exemplary contributions. But just because you like that treatment, does that mean everyone else does? Not at all. People should receive feedback—any kind of feedback—in a way that THEY wish to receive it—not the way that you like to receive it or give it. It's a reversal of the Golden Rule. How do we understand how people wish to be treated? We need to develop **appropriate** and **durable** relationships—that is the next hallmark of stewardship....

Who Do Your People Need You To Be Today?

We all need to ask this at various stages in our lives—as new parents, we should ask "Who does my baby need me to be right now? Who does my partner need me to be?" I asked that all the time as a new dad—often struggling with the answer! In turn, I have asked this often when my parents entered the twilight of their lives— "who does my mom need me to be at this moment?"

Great parents, great friends, great caregivers—they understand this question. It isn't about you. It's about the people you care about.

Same goes for leaders.

Your head isn't right? Tough night? Bad traffic? Missed deadlines? This or That?

Tough. Suck it up. What do your people need you to be today?

They may need you to be a hardass. They may need you to be a mentor. A listener. A coach. Whatever it is, **bring it**.

That's a hallmark of leadership and stewardship. Leader as Server.

I know what you may be thinking ... but what about you? Will someone be the person you need them to be?

Maybe. Hopefully.

But in the meantime, YOU be that person! It's a **selless** choice. Choose it.

Developing Relationships

Developing relationships is a key part of stewardship, and our relationships at work—whether with our leaders, our peers, or team members who report to us—are all key for us to understand how to navigate the way forward and establish our own leadership repertoire.

Of course, work relationships need to be appropriate; this is key. It's a major component of accepting that how people spend 80 percent of their lives is most certainly personal. However, it's not about pushing relationships that violate workplace boundaries or rules. Developing relationships is not about coercing people into spending social time with you or with their teammates! So many people seem to believe that the key to developing relationships with their teams is about taking everyone out for drinks or for lunch. Those things can be nice, but not everyone likes them (back to reversing the Golden Rule) and they have little to do with what we mean by developing true relationships at work—relationships that **grow trust**, **show respect,** and **build rapport**.

Key components of a successful relationship, regardless of the type, are trust, respect, and rapport. These elements need to be front of mind for any leader regardless of role or level. How do we grow trust, show respect, and build rapport? The recipe is simple, but not easy—it is rooted in time, observation, and communication. Let's explore each.

CHAPTER TWO

Grow Trust

"Trust is the highest form of human motiva-
tion. It brings out the very best in people."

—*Stephen Covey*

Trust is where it all begins and all ends. Growing and nurturing trust is the hallmark of any successful leader, parent, spouse, partner, friend—you name it. It is the hallmark of any successful relationship. Yet, despite this, we generally leave trust to chance. It simply evolves or doesn't evolve. If we earn someone's trust, it is generally through a series of interactions or evolutions that lead to a trusting relationship; however, those things are often not purposeful, intentful, or front of mind.

I ask leaders to consider this question: do your people trust you? And if you answer 'yes,' how do you know? What do you do to earn their trust every day? And what things might you do—accidentally or intentionally—that may erode that trust?

It is the same with parents, friends, and partners: does your child trust you, and do you nurture, grow and evolve that trust as they grow through the chapters of their lives? Trust changes at different stages of family relationships—expectations are very different now that my sons are in their 20s and driving their own lives forward. What is my role? Will I still accept stewardship, acknowledging that my position in their lives transcends a roof over their head and food on the table. Sure, I needed to do those things when they were little, but that made me a reliable parent, not necessarily a trustworthy one. Did my words match my actions? Was I credible in their eyes?

I always asked my boys to be kind to others, regardless of who they were. Apart from telling them, I knew it was important to demonstrate that to them. Smile. Say good morning to strangers. Help someone who needs it. Have lunch with the 'different' kid at school. Be respectful and kind to your teachers, classmates, custodians … everyone.

One afternoon in San Diego, I was on a conference call and was walking around the house with a headset on, talking away. My son Joon Ho was 9 or so and was playing with his Legos on the living room floor. The front door was open—pretty common in San Diego—and a few teens approached the front door. It looked like they were selling candy bars for school or something. I was caught up in my call, so just shook my head 'no' and pushed the door closed.

After I hung up, Joon Ho said, "Hey Daddy, that was rude." I stopped and looked at him, and asked "What was rude, Bud?" He went on to explain that I didn't have to close the door on those kids like that—that I could have paused my call for a moment—smiled, been polite, and asked them to return later.

He was absolutely right.

I was recalibrated by a 9-year-old.

Trusting relationships go both ways. Joon Ho trusted me enough to offer up a worthy correction. Damn, I couldn't imagine ever correcting my father. He was loving in many ways, but largely lived a "don't do as I do, do as I say" credo. If I would have shut Joon Ho down, told him it wasn't rude or offered some lame adult excuse, trust would have eroded a bit.

> *Sometimes trust dies right out from some monumental deception or lie—but often it is brought to its knees by hundreds of tiny little cuts.*

Relationships that are absent trust are frustrating, difficult, and often painful. If you have lost trust in a leader, a co-worker, a friend, or a partner, we will subconsciously default to negative assumptions, which only makes the relationship erode faster. If you don't trust your boss, and they say, "I have your best interests in mind," do you believe them? What if you don't trust your partner or spouse, and they say they are working late? Absent trust, you immediately default to 'They aren't working late—they are cheating or going out!'. Now, you may be right ... or they may actually be working late! It doesn't really matter, because absent trust, you'll likely default to the negative assumption. Distrust becomes a self-fulfilling prophecy.

So, how do we get ahead of this? The first thing we do is:

PUT TRUST FRONT OF MIND. Begin each day thinking ... what can I do today to build trust with the people around me?

• Spend quality time.

The finest gift we can give or receive is time. Everyone has the same amount, regardless of who they are, where they live, or what they do. Spending **quality** time with others builds trust because you become known to them. We are raised not to trust strangers. At work, it may be similar! As leaders, we need to become known to our constituency, as they become known to us. Absent these efforts, you may not be distrusted, but you may not have trust either. We can't successfully lead in this grey area—we need to make our trustworthiness clear.

Now, we all struggle with having enough time, and our management duties and tasks eat much of it before we know it. That's why leaders need to be purposeful in spending this rare commodity with their constituency ... and it's not about the **amount** of time, it's about the **quality** of time spent. I quickly learned that my frequent travel and time away from home had a distinct impact on the time that I spent with my sons and my wife, so I wanted to ensure that the time I did have to spend with them was of quality—time spent engaging, sharing, learning, and experiencing things together. 30 minutes of active engagement is far better than hours spent staring at my computer and my son staring at his iPad while we sit in the same room together.

Again, it's the same at work. Spending quality time with your team, your direct reports, your boss, or other members of your constituency isn't about volume. Sure, scheduled, hour-long one-on-ones can be valuable—but we only have so many hours to give. Focused, tuned-in check-ins of just a few minutes can make all the difference and is quality time well spent. Some of the best time spent when I was with Starwood Hotels was not necessarily the formal meetings or scheduled contact points, but the few minutes in the morning spent sharing a coffee with my boss, Joe, or one of my amazing peers on the team. Give the gift of quality time—even quality moments—and watch trust grow.

- **Observe, show interest, and build rapport.**

This component begins by being a successful observer. Watch for various physical and emotional cues that provide information to you regarding others. Transform these observations into an opportunity to build trust!

When people observe, and in turn show polite interest based on what they observe, they take steps to forming relationships, and thereby building trust.

For example, it is widely known among my close friends that I am a Cleveland Browns fan. It is a very tragic byproduct, as Cleveland fans will attest, from growing up in that part of the country. Browns fans are accustomed to the "maybe next year" approach to our beloved team's performance. So, when I wear Cleveland Browns attire, and someone comments in a cordial way, I am inclined to positively respond. If I walk into a pub and the bartender, upon observing my Browns attire, states, "Browns fan! Wow, I admire your dedication to your team! It hasn't been easy!" I immediately respond good-naturedly and engage positively, the first steps to building trust and rapport. However, if that same bartender ignores my attire—no rapport-building begins, and our engagement is simply another transaction in a long list of those that occur in the service industry. It's more damaging if they comment negatively— "The Browns huh? They suck!" Well, that will likely elicit a less-than-positive response, and we will be getting off on the wrong foot regarding trust, rapport or anything else!

That is a simple service example. In leadership, our ability to observe, show interest and build rapport is critical to developing relationships with our entire constituency. Leaders need to transcend simple surface niceties and put effort into engaging others.

The ubiquitous "how was your weekend?" or "how was your day off?" question is a simple yet salient example. It is asked in every workplace in any industry. It is generally answered with a "Fine, how was yours?" response. Neither party really cares—it is a social nicety that simply concludes itself without any real engagement.

Leaders need to use these simple interactions to ask better questions, learn more about their team members, and take the opportunity to show genuine interest!

Which interaction below do you think goes further into establishing trust and building rapport?

Leader: "How was your day off, Michael?"

Team Member: "It was great!"

Leader: "Good. Welcome back."

Leader: "How was your day off, Michael?"

Team Member: "It was great!"

Leader: "Excellent! What made it great?"

Team Member: "Well, my best friends and I ..."

Showing interest in what made it great for your team member is the part that matters here, whether it is something you would consider "great" or not! This isn't necessarily about finding common interest or agreement, it is about being empathetic and showing an interest in others. That is where rapport lives and where trust begins to grow. Your team member may love to work on cars and may go on to tell you about his restoration project—you may know nothing about cars, and that's ok. It's not about the cars—it's about you showing genuine interest in your team member's passion.

I remember as a young father how much joy I would take in my sons' laughter. It doesn't mean I always found whatever they laughed at funny ... I simply **took joy in their joy**. Just like I can take joy and find interest in other people's passions, whether I am passionate about the same thing.

Behavioral observation may be a bit trickier, but incredibly important as a tool in your leadership repertoire. It's all about active empathy. We often think of empathy as something we display when someone is feeling sad or upset, but let's consider it as a sort of **emotional radar**—what can I observe about a person's demeanor or attitude in any given moment? Are they happy about something? Confused? Angry? Dismissive? You could go on and on regarding the myriad of behaviors someone may show. The key is whether we can interpret them correctly through astute observation, and then show interest accordingly. It is a key component of emotional intelligence, called Social Awareness, and is critical to success as a leader—or as a person!

CHAPTER THREE

Self-Awareness and Our Capabilities

"Self-awareness is the bedrock of emotional intelligence"

—Daniel Goleman

The person in the mirror. Who do we see staring back? What are our own internal measures? Do you know what you're good at? Not so good at?

People who cannot identify their strengths struggle with self-awareness, just as those who cannot identify their weaknesses or deficiencies. Being aware of your strengths and weaknesses is only the first and easiest step. What we DO with this self-awareness is key, and directly ties with self-management as well. Being aware is a big step, but there is plenty left to do as a leader once that awareness is accepted and understood.

I struggle with patience, procrastination, engaging my mouth before my brain (a common extrovert disease), strategic planning (anything beyond a month is a mystery) and plenty of other things. It is a paradox of self-awareness that it is difficult to be self-aware by yourself—we need others to help provide feedback!

From my parents to my wife, from my colleagues to my kids, plenty have provided feedback on my actions and behaviors! The thing with loved ones, is they often have a high tolerance for our behaviors and quirks, so we need to be active in asking for feedback. It's not enough to simply ask "How do you perceive me?" or "How can I improve myself?" After all, general questions like that are easily answered with soft responses, and your friends, families, and colleagues will consciously or subconsciously route their answers through their various filters. Even if I ask my best friend, Frank, for his honest opinion, it will inevitably be put through his "best friend" filter, or my wife through her "this is the man I love" filter! These filters aren't bad ... in fact, they help keep any relationship in harmony to a certain degree. And as the old adage says, people who are brutally honest get more satisfaction from the brutality than the honesty.

As leaders, we need to seek feedback in more specific ways. We need to continue to ask great questions as mentioned earlier. We always have a debrief after every type of program that we do, whether it is a simple one-hour keynote or a three-day immersion program for leaders.

I used to simply state, "I think that went well!" and my team would generally agree. A generic statement begets a generic response. However, in the journey to be more self-aware, I work hard—emotionally hard—to identify areas for adjustment and improvement. So, rather than a macro "how did that go?" question, we need to go a bit deeper and truly call-out steps and missteps, wins as well as missed opportunities. For example, I may ask the team "Do you think I cut the discussion on self-management too short? I feel I may have done this segment a disservice ..." or something to that effect. Then, as a collective, we begin to ask more questions and encourage varied perspectives and opinions—all things that help us grow our self-awareness as leaders, and as people.

However, self-awareness is more than strengths and weaknesses, and the inevitable evolution that we trust such awareness brings. Another key component is understanding what emotions you are feeling, and why, at any particular time.

Our Emotions

What makes you angry? What makes you sad? What makes you happy? What makes you afraid? Understanding these four key human emotions—why we feel them and how they impact our behavior—is another crucial component of leadership and personal success. Only once we understand them can we then exercise the self-management elements that are so essential to anyone's leadership repertoire.

Anger

What makes you mad? Anger is very compelling! What triggers you? It is different for everyone. The first step to understanding your anger is accepting it as your OWN! No one or no thing makes you angry—**you** choose what makes **you** angry. Macro things like Injustice? Cruelty? Bigotry? Maybe micro things like traffic/road rage, people cutting lines, cheaters, liars ... the list could go on and on.

It isn't about getting rid of your anger. That would take medication or an internal peacefulness mechanism that I have certainly found elusive! It is about understanding it, acknowledging that it is there when it occurs, and then *taking command of it*, rather than letting it take command of you. Controlling this key emotion is critical for every leader ... every friend ... every person. And it is not easy.

It is interesting that the people nearest to us are often the source of our emotional triggers, and anger is no exception.

Our children, our family members, our dear friends—often they are the ones who seem to know how to trigger us; however, certain topics, ideas, or even a simple comment from a stranger can have a very real affect as well. I have one enduring trigger that has not gone away—it has simply morphed as I continue to work on my own self-awareness and self-management.

Growing up in a very traditional midwestern family, I was inadvertently raised as a homophobe. Not specifically—as my parents never said anything negative, or anything at all really, about sexuality. It was more my community and my friends—homosexuality was either ridiculed or something to be feared. Calling someone 'gay' was an insult or a joke—not a descriptor.

Becoming an adult and joining a larger community, my perspective certainly changed, but never more so until my oldest son, Ryan, approached me at the age of 15 to tell me that he was coming out. I didn't spend much time considering my sons sexuality up until that point. I will never forget our conversation, and vividly recall my immediate desire to show support and understanding to my son in every way that I possibly could. I told him that I would be the support he needed me to be—but the weight of how others felt about it didn't strike me until after he came out.

My 'anger' trigger then became rooted in others' comments about sexuality—anyone saying anything homophobic or insulting, instantly triggered me and made me angry. I would lash out at what I felt was their ignorance and bigotry. It led to verbal altercations in a variety of places, and I thought myself some type of crusader on behalf of my son. My reaction and responses made me dismissive at best, and combative at worse.

I shared with my son a particular interaction at an airport lounge—an interaction that simply left me calling someone an ignorant asshole. I asked him how he thought I should handle those kinds of situations— he shrugged and shared with me a great little piece of wisdom. He simply said, "Dad, didn't you once think the way they do? Didn't you make jokes and comments like that? You may not be able to change people with one conversation, but you can try."

I can try.

Maybe not call someone an ignorant asshole ... maybe instead try to make a difference in their minds. Acknowledge the anger, but don't project it out. Convert it to an internal mission, not an external confrontation.

The things that trigger us can often be small and simple, which makes those issues extra dangerous! In our personal lives, they can take so many forms, from bad traffic to rude manners. When my sons were little, they could trigger me in a second! Most parents understand this—we love our children with all our might, but no one can push our buttons like they do.

At work, it is equally important. Most of us will agree that the demonstration of anger at work is not conducive to most positive intended outcomes. Yet, from late arrivals at meetings to poor decisions, these metaphoric papercuts stack up. We need to recognize them as they are and how they make us feel, and then put them in their proper place—we will explore this in our next topic when we discuss Self-Management.

Sadness

What makes you sad? What frustrates you? Disappoints you? Occurrences of loss or grief that leave our hearts heavy are an emotional challenge that we will continue to face throughout the entirety of our lives. Sometimes they are significant things—the loss of a loved one is one most of us have shared. Sometimes they are small things—an unkind word or action, a missed opportunity or poor decision. Lastly, they may be enduring—a twinge of regret that brings sadness back when remembered.

I feel regret is the most complex form of sadness for me. I persevere to not carry it, yet we only realize it in hindsight, when it has already taken its subtle hold. Regret also can provide enduring and valuable lessons—it's the whisper in our minds that reminds us not to make the same mistake twice. Regret, in many ways, is emotional learning.

I remember coming home from school on weekends when I was at college. My father would ask me to join him for a beer, play a hand of cards, or just sit on the front steps and talk for a bit—but I seemed to always have other plans and more important things to do.

I loved my dad, that's for sure. But when we are in the prime of our young adult lives, we feel that we have all the time in the world, and that time is ours to be spent as we deem fit. At that time of my life, I didn't consider how others see time, especially my aging parents. It would have been so easy to stop for a moment and spend that time with my dad. It sucks that such wisdom often comes too late.

What I wouldn't give to go back in time and have that beer with him. To listen to his stories and see his smile...

Regret can be a heavy burden to bear, but it's real and it's there for a reason. It's teaching us something. Adjust. Consider your choices. Add context to the moment. When I hear people say they have no regrets, I wonder. You've never wanted to undo something that was done? Spent more time doing this or that? Share an extra kind word or withdraw a harsh one? Sounds like denial to me, and a lack of self-awareness.

The key to sadness born from regret is to learn from it. So, I don't simply lament the missed time with my dad; I manifested it in true quality time with my mom before dementia stole her mind. To this day, I cherish purposeful and wonderful moments with my sons—times full of laughter and love. And hours, days and any amount of time that I get to share with my wife Soledad—talking, eating, traveling, walking … or just being.

So, I thank my father for this gift of regret. Is it still a sadness in me? Sure. To call it anything else is to make it less. And if I had a time machine, I'd go back and spend those moments with him. Isn't that the very definition of regret? Nevertheless, I embrace this feeling, as it's helped make me the man I think my dad wanted me to become.

Fear

What makes you afraid? What thoughts haunt you? The doubts and dangers, real or imagined, that shake your confidence and cast shadows on your decisions and actions. Fear may be the most compelling human emotion. People who say they are "fearless" are generally posing; those who appear or behave fearlessly are actually overcoming their fear and choosing to act regardless, whether consciously or subconsciously. Fear is a 'good' emotion—it keeps us safe. However, it can also be limiting, and even debilitating.

Sadness and fear, like the other emotions, are as compelling as anger. It is not something we like to dwell on as people, so we often do not consider or contemplate the things that rally these emotions in us. Exploring sadness and anger **when you aren't currently feeling them** is a solid first step to self-awareness. Reflect on your feelings of loss, disappointment, frustration, or confusion—how did you deal with it then? I have found that, when embraced by emotions of sadness and/or fear, **the only way out, is through**. Accept the feeling as valid—even valuable; it makes you human and creates the foundation for your own feelings of empathy for others, and your own ability to process and deal with what you are feeling. No blame. No excuses. The key is to not let sadness or fear derail or consume you. That is, again, why self-awareness is so acutely attached to self-management.

It was December 5, 2019, when I landed in Wuhan, China—the first stop on a road trip that would take me to five cities throughout this interesting and engaging country and culture. I had been to China many times before, but not for this long of a trip. We were rolling out the signature two-day leadership program for a hotel client, which had been in design and development for over six months. We were thrilled to get it deployed to the leaders in the field!

I had no idea what that date would mean for me, the City of Wuhan, for China, and the world.

It was two delightful days with a hotel team that was so committed to the content and the leadership principles within the program. With material and presentation in both Mandarin and English, we quickly circumvented traditional barriers of language and culture and dove into the ideals that drive leadership success in any environment. From there, via train, we went on to Changsha, an ancient and beautiful city, on to Chongqing, an industrial powerhouse of over 28 million people, and then to Chengdu, the home of the Chinese Panda. The program ended just before the holidays in Shanghai, where I looked at 2020 ahead and considered all the work remaining for this wonderful group of hotels, as well as other organizations around the world. The horizon was bright with opportunity—2020 was going to be our best year yet.

Then the world began to change.

Whispers out of Wuhan, at first. Then, throughout eastern China. A SARS-like virus again? No one had a clue at the time. We were sure things would be OK. I returned to Asia in early February to continue the rollout that we started in China, this time to the Philippines. I had bought N-95 masks at Home Depot before I left to bring along with me, as a volcano had erupted in the Philippines and colleagues in Manila were concerned about the ash in the air. I still look back at that blissfully ignorant time, not having a clue how those colleagues may eventually make use of those masks and the others I brought along.

I remember speaking to the Vice President of Human Resources in Hong Kong, where my client was based. I was to go there after the completion of the programs in the Philippines, to debrief the rollout to date, as well as to pilot a new brand program that we had just completed. I remember her words so clearly.

"Go home while you can Louis. This outbreak in China is something serious."

I booked the next flight to the States, still thinking that it was a small hiccup in Asia that would quickly be dealt with. Asia is resilient. Asia is strong. From tsunamis to hurricanes, from reactor meltdowns to political strife, this region always continues on.

Then the world began to unravel.

First, Asia. Then, Europe. Then, the US. Travel stopped. Hospitality stopped. Everything stopped.

We went from looking forward to our brightest year to wandering confused and uncertain through our darkest year. Sad? Distraught? Frustrated? It came in inches every day. Relentlessly.

Anger made a visit as well ... and I don't recall being angry at anything in particular, which made it even more difficult to grapple with. Being mad at the pandemic seemed useless and even childish, yet anger often does bring about childlike behavior.

All of this, combined with the very real health and safety issues that I harbored for my family and friends—especially those at risk for various reasons— contributed to this compression of emotions.

No one was exempt from the impact of the pandemic; it truly touched us all. Regardless of its universal scope, would it have brought anyone comfort if the virus took form and stated …

"Hey, don't take this personally. I'm a virus. Sure, I killed your loved one, hospitalized a few others, made your job evaporate, and shook the structure of your society. But it isn't personal."

Fuck you, Covid.

Just like everything else, this was personal, as it impacted me and everyone else personally!

From a leadership perspective, it put many of us on notice. It is easy to lead in the proverbial sunlight—when everything is going well, and challenges are made up of the beautifully usual and simply mundane. The measure of your leadership—like the measure of your relationships—is not how to lead, act, or behave when everything is easy … it is how you do it when things are dark and difficult. When people are afraid. When you are afraid.

And there is no magic bullet. No defined series of steps. No simple mental trick. Things like understanding the stages of grief, mental tricks to diffuse anger or sadness, or even the physiology of intense emotions like endorphins and adrenaline may add context or structure to what we are feeling as leaders. This certainly may assist in our logical processing of what we may be faced with at a particular time. But taking you, the leader … the parent … the friend … to a place where your anger, sadness, or fear needs to be overcome so you can make good decisions and be the person that your people need you to be at any given moment, is uniquely within you.

It begins and ends with attitude and perspective. Accept the emotion, take it as yours, and again, start asking great questions, this time of yourself.

I was sitting in our empty office, wondering what to do next with myself. I was lucky that my wife had decided to go forward and expand in the restaurant business that she had started many years before we met—and we now had two new locations opening right after Covid began to take its hold on the world. I know it would seem that opening restaurants as the pandemic was beginning to rage was the distinct opposite of 'lucky'—more like tragic!

However, these fast-casual restaurants were located on two military installations, and the military didn't close. I poured my time and energy into their respective openings, which blissfully kept my mind off my evaporated hospitality consultancy.

So, they were open, and running, and there I was back in my office continuing in my sulk. No more distractions. Now what?

The hand-drawn picture on my bulletin board brought about a melancholy smile. It was drawn for me by the daughter of the Human Resources Director at the hotel where I was training in Wuhan six months earlier. It seemed like forever ago.

The team at that hotel spoke very little English. All our materials were in English and Mandarin, and I had a bi-lingual co-facilitator assisting. Along the way, there was plenty of pantomime and gestures to drive our leadership points home. I have always been a believer that there are a million ways to communicate, only one is with your voice.

At the end of the program, the HR Director handed me this picture from her daughter, who visited the class briefly with her mom the day before. It was a classic kid-drawn picture ... with smiling faces, a big sun in the sky and big heads!

I asked why she drew me this picture. My co-facilitator translated, stating that the little girl said that your class made her mom happy, so that made her happy, and she wanted to say thank you with this picture. And then came the tears ... and the hug ... and that she was the one making me happy. And to think what they were going through in Wuhan now.

Time to soldier up and stop looking at the walls. I reached out to my colleagues and friends around the world. How can we help? How can we work together and help our hotels, our restaurants, and our industry get through this? We didn't ask for any fee ... hell, no one had a dime to spend anyway.

We gladly helped with video conferences with hotels in markets around the world, carrying a message of pragmatic (not toxic) optimism as they faced new challenges every day. This effort kept relationships strong, the leadership voice loud, and the messages of trust, respect, and relationships flowing. After all, this was personal for everyone.

We need to ask ourselves internal questions when these emotions rush in at breakneck speed. "What does this anger, fear, or sadness tell me? What do I do with it? Will it serve me well in my role as a leader (or a partner, parent, son/daughter, or friend) to project this emotion outward? If I do, what are the consequences? What is my intended outcome?"

Instill confidence or reinforce trepidation?

Seek a way forward or hide in the shadows?

Make an argument worse or find reconciliation?

The questions in your mind will vary depending on the circumstance ... the key is to ask them. Then, act on your answers. During the pandemic, I turned to pragmatic optimism over toxic positivity. Everything isn't ok right now, and we lack answers and struggle with an uncertain future, but as a team (or family, or neighborhood) we are presented with opportunities to do so much good. Let's help others. Let's be kind. Let's do our part to ease other's anger, fear, and sadness even as we deal with our own. Let's commit to improving this human condition through action AND attitude ...

… and let's not forget these lessons that we have learned—about not just what to do, but more so how to BE—when the darkness clears, and the sun returns. Let's choose to be at our best not only when the world is at its worst. Let's choose it all the time.

Happiness

I saved happiness for last for a reason. Not because it is the easiest to accept, rejoice in, and manifest. After all, we all want to be happy, right?

Of course we do, yet we often outsource our happiness to the outside world. That is to say, we seek happiness through external sources or our experience and interaction with things or endorphin producers such as social media posts and our number of 'likes' or 'followers.' We understand how our engagement with the right people can bring us happiness, and rightfully so. But we don't often see happiness as something derived within us—something we create for ourselves—and that may be the very best source. So where does happiness come from?

It comes from our gradual success with our journey with the other three. Anger. Sadness. Fear.

When you understand your anger. Your sadness. Your fear. When you channel these powerful emotions appropriately, astutely, and healthily, you open the door to your own happiness.

Things don't make you happy. An enlightened self-awareness makes you happy—and gives you the critical tools to be a successful leader, and a successful, content, at-peace person.

CHAPTER FOUR

Mastering Emotional Intelligence

*"Mastering others is strength. Mastering
yourself is true power."*

—*Lao Tzu*

Self-Management

Are you the master of your own behavior?

Self-management is acutely tied to self-awareness. No leader
can be effective without a firm grip on both of these crucial
elements of emotional intelligence.

If self-awareness is the journey to a true understanding of
yourself, then self-management is the journey to adept and
prudent control of that understanding, and how we demonstrate
it to the outside world.

Our society and our world are rife with examples of intelligent people behaving badly—not self-managing—and thereby negatively impacting themselves and those around them, often to deadly consequences.

Something as mundane as losing your temper over someone cutting you off on the highway ... or as severe as destroying a personal relationship over your inability to resist lust and temptation ... are all examples of the inability to self-manage. Clearly, these issues can have a significant impact on our professional environment as well.

I was enjoying a glass of wine with a colleague. It had been a full day at our annual conference, and these social gatherings at the end of the day were always a great opportunity to socialize, discuss the matter of the day, eat some great food, network, grow relationships, and have fun!

Sometimes too much fun.

Add an open bar to any event, and people find themselves challenged regarding self-management. A few drinks can be great fun, but a few too many is legendary for impairing people's judgement—that is to say, their ability to self-manage. This event was no exception.

My colleague, who was a senior executive at the organization, was chatting with me about the conference thus far. I was the head of Human Resources at that time, so we often had plenty to talk about. The band was playing all the great cover songs from the past few decades, and everyone loved the music ... especially one particular couple.

They were having a great time, dancing like they were the only ones on the dance floor—touching and grinding like no one was watching. One was a senior member of management, the other person his direct subordinate. Other people on and off the dance floor were casting curious glances at least—and outright staring in disbelief at worse.

Oh, and they were married ... and not to each other.

We stood there watching two people dance their way to an unintended outcome, as I am confident that they didn't come to this corporate event earlier in the evening with the intent to demonstrate behaviors that would likely impact them both professionally and personally. But that's what can happen when we fail to self-manage.

Leaders behaving badly is not uncommon. Not just leaders, of course. Politicians, athletes, musicians and so many people in the public arena have seen their careers ruined, or at least damaged, from the exhibition of "bad behavior" manifested through tantrums, losing their temper, the ability to resist a myriad of temptations, you name it.

We are all constantly dealing with our ability to self-manage. Struggles—even battles—with procrastination, timeliness, temperament, attitude, bias, and a myriad of other manifestations of our behavior are examples of our daily self-management challenges.

Leaders face subtle forms of self-management like these regularly. Overlooking a team member's performance issue, simply hoping it will go away? Judging a colleague's intent without due diligence or consideration? Demonstrating behaviors that will negatively impact those around us? Please, those without these sins go ahead and cast that stone. We have all been there.

What we need to do is put our need to self-manage front of mind. Always. And challenge ourselves: How should I respond in this circumstance? If I yell ... scream ... berate... it may feel good in the moment, but will it serve me well when the dust settles? The answer is almost always NO. But as we have learned, emotions are very compelling ... so how do we get a handle on the boogeyman of self-management?

Pause—Reflect—Act

Self-management is first about controlling impulses. As leaders ... and as people ... we often react in the moment rather than consider our actions or behavior. What results is often regret over what we did or said—the classic moment when you realize, in hindsight, that your reaction and/or response didn't result in something positive!

When we feel these emotional moments—moments of anger, surprise, confusion, confrontation, you name it—rather than simply react, we need to pause, reflect (even for a moment), and then choose our response or action with this reflection in mind.

The magic question we ask ourselves in this moment of pause and reflection is this:

Will this response that I am about to bring to my immediate world serve me well in its aftermath?

Will it make the situation worse or better?

Will it positively or negatively impact my ability to be an effective leader, parent, spouse, or friend?

Sure, sometimes the immediate, negative, harsh, confrontational response *feels good* in the moment after it is delivered ... the middle finger to the guy who cut you off ... the harsh comment to a customer or colleague ... the blistering retort to someone because they are on your last fucking nerve ... but will it serve you well in the aftermath?

One of my favorite sayings from my dad comes to mind ...

> *"Son, don't wrestle in the mud with pigs. You both get muddy, and the pig likes it."*

My dad always called it "taking the high road." What he was talking about was an element of self-management.

Easier said than done, right? That's true. So how can we stack the odds in our favor? Always consider your Intended Outcome.

Intended Outcome

Everything we do ... every action, comment, decision, or directive ... has an outcome and/or consequence. As leaders, we need to put this outcome **front of mind** in the form of **intended outcome**. As you begin an interaction, make a decision, plan a course of action, always consider this first: what is my intended outcome? What result do I want from this action or interaction? That is to say, what outcome will best serve my constituency, the person or persons I am interacting with, and myself!

Once you determine your intended outcome, your behaviors and actions should be dedicated to driving toward that outcome! It could be very specific, or sometimes a bit more general, but powerful, nonetheless.

Consider this. When you get up in the morning, do you want it to be a great day or an awful day? Great day, I would think (and hope) most of us would say. Then, in a macro sense, it is your intended outcome for the day to be great! In that case … **BEHAVE ACCORDING TO THAT INTENTION**! Bring the attitude, interaction, perspective, and engagement that would contribute to the day being positive and successful. Drive toward your intended outcome with purpose and try to stack the deck in your metaphoric favor.

Now, that may be in the macro sense … an approach to a day, a week, or any measure of time. The same applies to any interaction or decision. Hosting a team meeting? A morning briefing? A training session? What is your intended outcome from any of these events? Consider the end result that you want, and then build your actions and behaviors around this end result. That is keeping intended outcome front of mind.

It is equally powerful in unexpected or sudden situations. Regardless of the circumstance, we retain the power to choose and consider an intended outcome. Let's say you get pulled over by the police when you are rushing to get home. Your emotions kick in as the officer approaches your window. What is your intended outcome from the interaction that is about to happen? An interaction that you didn't plan or want to happen. You have an outcome in mind nevertheless, right? DON'T GET A TICKET! So, what do you do in that circumstance? Do you tell the officer to leave you alone and go find a real crime? Will that approach lead to your intended outcome of 'no ticket'? Not a chance, right? You adjust your attitude, self-manage, and bring the most polite and contrite attitude, words, and demeanor that you can in the hope of getting a warning rather than a citation—you are working toward your intended outcome.

I would rush phone calls from my parents back in the day. I was always busy doing something or another, so would always be polite, but very short and concise. Sometimes that may have been necessary in the moment, but there were plenty of times that it wasn't. I would treat those calls like an interruption to my day.

I would love to get a call from my dad now, but that won't happen since he passed so long ago. Now, this isn't another regret story, this is an intended outcome story! I learned another valuable lesson. When my mother calls, what is my intended outcome for that call, regardless of the topic of conversation? I want my mother to feel attended to, cared for, and loved. So, I behave accordingly on that call to reach that intended outcome. It is the same for my sons, my lovely wife, Soledad, my dear friends. With colleagues and clients, I want them to feel heard, I want to understand their message and their needs, and provide any help or assistance that I can. Once again, that is my intended outcome, regardless of the topic of the conversation. Move toward it, and it fills every interaction and action with meaning.

Now, there are also unintended outcomes. Outcomes that are derived from our actions or behaviors that we don't purposefully move toward yet occur anyway. Unintended outcomes are common when we don't exercise self-management. We hurt someone's feelings, damage a relationship, or cause harm in some way ... we didn't "mean to do it" perhaps, but it happened anyway. It is an unintended outcome. A consequence. And, whether we intended it or not, we need to own it.

I always repeated this tried-and-true quote to my sons—*"you are free to choose, but you are never free of the consequences of your choice!"* That's all about intended and unintended outcomes. Like my traffic stop example earlier ... no one sets out with the intent to get a traffic ticket (that would be odd), but if you speed, or drive while texting, or whatever, you certainly run that risk. It may not be your intention, but if it happens, it's yours to own. It's not the officer's fault, and it's not the fault of circumstance. It's your fault. It may be an unintended outcome, but it's yours to own.

All too often, we try to hide or cover in our lack of **intent** when a particular outcome occurs.

"I didn't mean for that accident to happen!"

"I didn't mean to hurt their feelings!"

"I didn't mean to show disrespect."

Well, let's hope not. If you intended a negative or harmful outcome, that's generally a different discussion. However, if your actions, words, or approach resulted in this unintended outcome nevertheless, we as leaders need to own it. Not lament over it. Not wring our hands about it. Just own it.

Once we own it, we need to reflect on it. That's where the learning lives. Because on reflection, we may begin to understand why or how something we said or did had a negative/unintended outcome. We can then adjust and behave or act differently next time. Our reflection on our behavior and self-management helps us grow and develop our self-awareness.

In the spirit of reflection, I'd like to look back on what we discussed earlier in the book regarding Trust and Respect, as these two key elements are a great foundation for all our Intended Outcomes.

When considering your approach, demeanor, or action, use Trust and Respect to gut-check your intended outcome: will what I am about to say or do actively build trust? Will it demonstrate respect, even in a subtle way? If not, is that part of my intended outcome? Will it serve me well in the long term?

And on the topic of 'long term.' Look, I am a realist and like to think I am pragmatic, and I am certainly abundantly human. Are there times when your intended outcome, at least in the moment, is to wound, insult, or 'get back' at someone? Be snide? Be clever? "I'll show this asshole ..."

Sure. On occasion. Just remember. If that's your intended outcome. And you get it. What's the long-term impact? Harm a relationship? Maybe. Put an insensitive idiot in their place? Could be. Just remember, be prepared to own the consequences, whatever they may be. And remember what I said earlier, about wrestling in the mud with pigs!

> *"There can be no knowledge without emo-*
> *tion. We may be aware of a truth, yet until*
> *we have felt its force, it is not ours. To the*
> *cognition of the brain must be added the*
> *experience of the soul."*
>
> —*Arnold Bennett*

CHAPTER FIVE

Developing Others

*"The finest gift we can give is to recognize
the gifts within others."*

Recognizing gifts in others. What does that mean exactly?

As leaders, every person on our team, whether subordinate, peer, or superior, has their gifts. They may be obvious and straightforward—they may be latent and difficult to discern—but they are there.

Successful leaders have a certain radar. An ability to identify underutilized strengths—or even to see perceived weaknesses as a gift of their own. Everything has a lesson ... if we are willing to learn it.

We should consider those around us with a new lens. What gifts do they have that they may not even recognize? Is it patience? Perhaps spirit? Tenacity? Resilience? Empathy? The ability to listen? The ability to tell stories? So many gifts that seldom manifest themselves on resumes or get reflected in an annual review. Still, these gifts are fertile soil to grow talent and team, and recognizing them goes a long way to developing relationships, building trust, and demonstrating respect.

Not only do leaders recognize gifts, but they also help remove barriers. The kinds of barriers that we may often build within ourselves.

Whether it is a feeling of inability, uncertainty, incapability, or the tried-and-true comfort zone, leaders help others assuage those fears, providing the coaching and encouragement they need to move forward, take risks, and extend themselves beyond their own perceived limitations.

Fear of failure can be debilitating. Leaders understand that fear in all its bravado or subtlety, and help people work past it. Not unlike a parent who helps a child overcome a fear or trepidation to try something new—the inclination to not take even a simple risk can change the trajectory of your personal and professional life in ways we never fully understand.

It's coaching, in a way, although coaching in our professional environment seems to generally be task-related—whether someone exceeds a particular expectation or misses the mark, we want to recognize their success or get them back on track. Important efforts, to be sure. No different than a coach in any sport working to hone an athlete's ability to be successful in that particular endeavor. However, applying a deeper lens, beyond the task, effort, or role at hand, is a different effort—an effort steeped in stewardship.

It certainly takes an extra commitment from the leader. It is grounded in truly caring about the people that you work with, rather than seeing them as only a way to hit a target or achieve a goal.

Look, I am a realist. We need to achieve whatever metrics we are striving for, that is for sure. We are at work for a reason. But when we consider the challenges and strengths that our teammates have with a lens **beyond the task** or job description, we set up the individual, the team, and the organization for far more success in both the near and short term. Loyalty, commitment, camaraderie, and performance grow exponentially.

I grew up a stutterer.

That's wrong, really. I still am a stutterer, or a PWS (person who stutters), an acronym common in the stuttering community.

In my childhood, it was debilitating. My self-esteem was consistently in tatters. That is why I see it as something 'then' and not so much 'now.' Nevertheless, it remains a very real part of me.

When I was in grade school, my stutter was an ongoing angst-driving pain in the ass. Speech therapy didn't help much ... the therapists were old school and just seemed to make things worse. I was lucky to have a wonderful cadre of friends that never made fun of my speech (Sam, Kevin, Dale, Scott, Joe ... you know who you are) but there was never a shortage of insensitive assholes who couldn't wait to make a porky pig comment, tell me to "spit it out," or things much worse.

Despite my stutter, I was a pretty gregarious and outgoing kid, despite my fears to speak. I would dread the moments in school when we each had to read a paragraph aloud, and hated myself when I knew the answer, but didn't raise my hand in fear that the answer would never get across my lips, not without frustration, embarrassment, and giggles from my classmates. I would fake illness ... I even made myself throw up in class once so I would get sent to the nurse ... because that was better than speaking out loud.

I finally had a therapist that was new. She was young, kind, and not like the other therapist who would make me do these verbal drills that just felt painful. I remember meeting with her—I was in 4th grade.

"Let's talk," she said.

I stared at her and said, "I can't."

"Let's find a way," she said.

That day shifted my entire life.

She introduced me to an approach that she called 'AS,' which stands for Avoidance and Substitution. To summarize, I practiced avoiding certain letter combinations and substituting other words and synonyms for those that presented an ongoing or immediate difficulty for me. Some combinations were always a challenge, some would come out of nowhere. But this technique worked like magic for me. I would ask my mother to pass me the water, for example, and the 'w" in water just wouldn't come. I'd say "wa ... wa ... wa ... wa ..." and just get stuck. Then, I would pause and say "glass" or "cup" or "drink" instead of 'water,' and it would come right out.

Where is the hidden gift in this story? Was it my ability to become a walking thesaurus full of synonyms? No. My therapist said she recognized my gregarious nature and knew that we just needed to find a way to let it flow. She noticed me laughing, being silly, and playing on the playground with anybody I could find. So many other kids in speech therapy sadly spent time alone or in very small groups. She said that my innate extroversion was my gift.

I found that strange. I thought I was just comfortable being the clown.

Of course, it was my intended outcome to fully put my stutter in the rearview mirror now that I had my 'trick'! The universe had other plans, of course. When I went out for the 9th-grade play and got the lead role, it wasn't my intended outcome to fail and drop out of the cast. But I did. I over-extended my ability to control my stutter, and as a result, I disappointed a lot of people, including myself. Our drama coach and teacher were amazing, redirecting my efforts to stage management and student directing, channeling another gift I didn't know I had that she explained to me—she called it "stick-to-it" and grit. I see it now as perseverance.

I still stutter to this day. In nearly every sentence that leaves my mouth. I continue to avoid and substitute words, and this approach works for me to the extent that I now speak for a living. Despite all the practice I have had over the years, I still stutter on occasion when I present or facilitate, and even more so in casual conversation, but it isn't the boogeyman it once was. My perseverance drives me forward, no matter how often I stumble.

Call to action, leaders! Whether it is a formal review process, weekly one-on-one, or just a morning catch-up over coffee, consider your teammates from this nuanced perspective. What traits or behaviors do they display that they may be able to leverage to make them even more successful? Also, what are those that may be holding them back? As we mentioned before, a lack of self-confidence, unreasonable risk aversion, unrecognized barriers, and other elements can depress even the brightest talent.

CHAPTER SIX

Developing Leadership Credibility

*"Credibility is a leader's currency. With it,
the leader is solvent. Without it, the leader
is bankrupt."*

—*John Maxwell*

Leadership Credibility

The elements we discuss in this book are key components of leadership credibility. In an effort to articulate this for the leaders that we work with, Inspire Consulting Group developed a model to express it succinctly. This two-part model reflects the essential elements that make up leadership credibility:

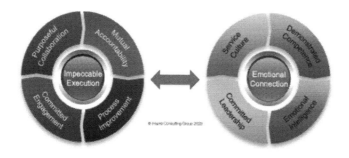

Both components are equally important. If a leader only succeeds in executing impeccably, without true regard for their people, then success will be short-lived. Conversely, if a leader forms emotional connections at every level, but does not execute and deliver operational excellence, they are not much of a business partner at all.

Impeccable Execution

The elements of Impeccable Execution all contain the same DNA as every message resident in this book—**intent** and being intentful in our actions and behaviors. Putting the elements of Accountability, Process Improvement, Engagement and Collaboration front of mind—daily—with an eye toward an intended outcome is the recipe.

A key component of leadership credibility is about being an **Exemplary Business Partner**—and that partnership is more poignant now more than ever...

> *"It may only be a matter of time before AI does your job faster, better, more efficiently and, most of all, less expensively."*

> *This was a senior executive speaking to a ballroom full of finance directors. You could have heard a pin drop.*

He went on to explain further, stating that those in attendance needed to see AI as not a replacement for them, but as an extra pair of hands, as it were. AI should help them be better. However, in order to do that, these finance professionals needed to make themselves indispensable to their constituency. Investors, corporate executives, general managers, colleagues, direct reports—all need to see you as not people who simply make the numbers dance. AI will soon do that. They need to see you as true partners.

My workshop was next.

The goal of this workshop was straightforward, although the aforementioned set-up felt a bit ominous. I had three hours to impart the fundamentals needed for these financial professionals to begin to become exemplary business partners and grow their leadership credibility beyond their technical capability.

So, with that premise in mind, we developed the Exemplary Business Partner workshop founded on our Leadership Credibility model, with the intrinsic elements that any leader needs to develop that partnership. After all, that's what all leaders should aspire to be. However, *wanting it* and *being it* is the rub, isn't it? Throughout my Human Resources career, HR people were always clamoring for a 'seat at the table,' and when they'd get it—with elevated roles, titles, and responsibilities— they often still dwelled in their vertical, never truly engaged in the commercial or operational aspects of the business. We quickly learned that being a business partner isn't merely an intellectual game, it's a relationship game, with intellectual and operational elements endemic throughout.

We centered this Exemplary Business Partner workshop on the four elements within Impeccable Execution from the Leadership Credibility model. We touched on the Emotional Connection aspects as well, but the real exploration was on the execution elements for this particular workshop—a great first effort into getting these aspects front of mind for these financial professionals.

Let's take a look at each of these elements and how they fit together in the credibility model.

Mutual Accountability

Silos are a problem in so many organizations. We naturally get focused on our own responsibilities, results, P&Ls, problems, successes, and so on. We may inadvertently reflect on our job descriptions and what we are here to do, and gradually form a myopic view of our business—we focus on our function or department, losing touch with the fact that we are part of a greater whole.

On the road to mutual accountability, we need to discover the answer to many salient questions: how do **our** efforts impact **your** efforts? If we achieve (or don't achieve) a particular milestone or objective, how does that impact your business unit or function? Perhaps most importantly, we never lose sight of the fact that we both want the same ultimate intended outcome—an acceptance of shared success and shared failure.

In Mutual Accountability, we also examine our shared constituencies, and how we all contribute to how that constituency assesses our shared value. The real understanding on how we are accountable to each other—and how we play a role in each other's success and failure—is a key component of Impeccable Execution and a valuable exploratory exercise on the road to being an Exemplary Business Partner.

Process Improvement

We are creatures of habit, and easily get caught up in our routines. Work processes are no different. Whether it's an unwritten work 'rule' or formalized Standard Operating Procedure, we are not inclined to innovate, change, challenge or improve them. Why not? Well, they are not front of mind. We don't approach our processes with the intent to assess and improve them, we approach our processes as a part of our provided infrastructure in our particular environment.

Many of us are often subjected to various processes and procedures outside of our work environment and notice the opportunity for process improvement! Who hasn't been in a retail environment, government office, airport, or other similar institution and thought "there has got to be a better way!" The people that operate those environments are stuck in the same mindset as we are in our professional environments: the "that's just the way it is" mindset.

We often need to move out of our vertical responsibilities in order to break out of that mindset and bring about process improvement, all in the spirt of the other three elements of accountability, engagement and collaboration. Considering growing trust and our ongoing efforts to build and develop our relationships, we need to ask others outside of our particular areas of responsibility for their perspective with an outsider's eye. "I would love your thoughts on how this could be improved," is not only a great way to assess your processes from a different perspective, but also a way to mature your relationship with your colleagues.

The other opportunity is to not only ask for the outsider's perspective, but the insiders as well. Speaking with people that are part of the process and impacted by it are a great resource for improvement opportunities—if asked the right questions in the right way.

Our intended outcome was simple. Improve the process in housekeeping by asking them what innovations, ideas or changes they could brainstorm! It made perfect sense: engage those that do the job with the challenge of how to improve their processes and actions. We gathered them all into a ballroom, presented what we were hoping to achieve, and then asked them to brainstorm ideas. We thought we were being extra clever by doing the presentation in different languages and multi-lingual visual aids.

We came up with nothing. The room attendants seemed disinterested—even a bit bothered. We were feeling kind of dejected—we thought for sure that by including them in the process improvement discussion, we would not only achieve our intended outcome, but also make inroads into building trust and fostering collaboration.

We thought right—we just went about it wrong.

We quickly learned that we needed to look at this effort from a different perspective. Bringing these room attendants into a ballroom with a presentation and report-out format was a mistake. It created an uncomfortable, way-out-of-comfort-zone vibe that certainly wasn't conducive to idea generation or active sharing. We reverted to one of our early cornerstones in this book—treat people the way THEY want to be treated.

We learned from that mistake quickly and changed up the approach. We went into the Housekeeping Department, gathered in small groups of four or five room attendants around a housekeeping cart, and asked great questions. "What would you take away from the cart that you don't use or is ineffective?" "What would you add to your cart that would make your job easier?" "How would you rearrange your cart?" Great conversations started— leading to other salient questions and discussions— which led to effective and impactful changes to both process and procedure.

By bringing in the elements of Committed Engagement, Mutual Accountability, and Purposeful Collaboration, we achieved our intended outcome of Process Improvement.

We quickly learned that the four pillars of Impeccable Execution seldom stand alone. Each pillar works in harmony with the other three—they are often crucial to one another in order to be successful.

Committed Engagement

Committed Engagement is communication centered. It is a key component of Impeccable Execution, as we cannot execute without both an intentful *communication* strategy, as well as an intentful *engagement* strategy.

As with the other elements, our communication often simply transpires, and it is often done with the goal of sending a particular message or to share certain information. It often is not done with the intent to actively and purposefully engage, assure understanding, and nurture the other core elements of accountability, process improvement, and collaboration.

So, when we communicate as leaders, we must actively consider the related engagement aspects and what that engagement means for us to clearly articulate the goal or objective, give, and receive feedback, and share ideas and variable perspectives. If not, we are merely a human bulletin board, pushing out data that may be music to our own ears, but may be misunderstood noise to others.

Purposeful Collaboration

Collaboration is king. Few organizations will dismiss the importance of individuals and teams working together. However, collaboration usually occurs out of a singular need, or even in moments of desperation. For instance, when an individual or team is in critical need of assistance, other members might step in to help. Although collaboration is always seen as an effort to work together, it isn't often seen as an effort to **think** together. So, the cavalry charges in, helps the individual or team in need, and then returns to their own world once the problem is solved. Collaboration? Sure. Purposeful collaboration? Not so much.

The goal behind Purposeful Collaboration is not only to work together in moments of desperation or dire need but also to collaborate as a matter of course, leading to many beneficial ends! To grow trust, demonstrate respect, build relationships, share accountability, and, of course, solve problems and evolve your business.

That is where the thought collaboration element enters. Working together not on a physical task or effort, but collaborating on problem-solving, idea generation, process improvement, and every other aspect of credible leadership. The finest plans, ideas, and solutions are born from this level of collaboration. And, as the word purposeful would suggest, you **seek** it, you don't wait for it.

"We simply can't fulfill the leadership needs we have with the aggressive growth that is ahead, at least not internally. Even if we go outside the organization, it will be a challenge, as every hotel company is expanding within the market."

It was 2016. I was having a conversation with the General Manager of Le Meridien Saigon in Vietnam. We were discussing the parameters of our upcoming leadership retreat for his team, and the topic of growth throughout the Vietnam/Cambodia market came up. He went on to share the current number of hotels in the pipeline throughout the region and emphasized the need for hundreds of senior leaders to staff those hotels in the coming years. While the infrastructure at Marriott was broad and robust, it lacked a market-specific tactical program to identify, develop, and deploy high-performing talent within a rapidly growing market.

*Thought collaboration ensued, a solution evolved, and **Accelerate** was born.*

It took nearly nine months for Accelerate to come to be. We worked with operators at different levels within Marriott, external program designers at ICG, and other *thought leaders who were experts in the Learning & Development field. This was true collaboration at every level with one goal in mind: how do we develop and deploy a program that purposefully meets our intended outcome of effectively growing quality, capable and prepared senior leaders **fast**? There were wonderful tertiary outcomes of trust building, relationship development, talent retention, job satisfaction—the list went on.*

And we had one chance to get it right. If it failed, the market would be instantly behind the curve.

*We began design in earnest, developing a year-long program that would develop high-potential leaders throughout the market. These junior leaders would then enter the program, christened **Accelerate.** The program was multi-faceted and multi-experienced, with a comprehensive curriculum that included collective learning as a unified group, field application of new skills and behaviors, temporary reassignment to different hotels and functions, peer and leader mentoring, and ongoing assessment and follow-up.*

The General Managers were charged with identifying the participants for the program through a vetting process that included past performance, skill, and—perhaps most of all—desire and zeal. We worked closely as we vetted their selection process, and they vetted our content development. All this happening in two different countries on two different continents—years before 'Zoom' was in everyone's vocabulary.

We brought the program to market in 2017 with two full classes of participants. These were local leaders from Vietnam and Cambodia—not expatriates. They were hungry and so were we! I traveled to Vietnam to deliver the classroom segments and to assist the local team in the macro-administration of the program. We collaborated closely with the hotel teams, each of them committed to providing the best possible learning and work experience for these engaged young leaders.

The program was an initial success based on the feedback from participants, mentors, and hotel teams, but the real proof would be in whether it truly prepared these junior leaders for roles of greater responsibility.

Accelerate ran for three years, until Covid reared its ugly head and ground everything to a halt. People who participated in the program were being promoted at an exciting rate, but no telling what the pandemic was going to do to everyone's career, not just those in the program.

Fast forward to 2023, where I had the honor of doing a regional conference for Intercontinental Hotel Group (IHG) in Hanoi. While there, I recognized a face at the evening reception. It was a young man who was a junior accountant that participated in the Accelerate program in 2018. He was now the Director of Finance for a major resort for IHG. It was wonderful to catch up—we both still had pictures and videos on our phones from our Accelerate sessions together. He fondly reflected on his time in the program, and how it helped him have the skills and the confidence to move forward. He was living proof that the program worked.

More so, he was living proof that when people collaborate with purpose to achieve a goal, they are exponentially more suited to reach that goal than well-intended people with different efforts driving in general directions.

When we finished with the workshop for these wonderful finance professionals, they left with an understanding of the importance of the elements of Impeccable Execution and their need to develop relevant, lasting partnerships with their constituency. We all need to do our technical tasks well, whatever they may be, and a job well done should bring any practitioner of their chosen skill joy and satisfaction.

We soon learn, however, that it isn't only **what we do**, but **who we are when we do it**, that matters so very much. That's what people are loyal to. That's what builds trust and relationships. That's what people remember.

Your legacy will never be your spreadsheets—it will always be your leadership.

.

CONCLUSION

"Persevere every day to have the heart of a lion, the skin of a rhino, and the soul of an angel."

One of my favorite movies is *The Princess Bride*—a popular favorite for many! I enjoy it on so many levels, whether it be the comedic parts or the dramatic elements. I found especially poignant the interaction of the princess when she is engaging with the dread pirate Roberts, who she doesn't realize is actually her long lost love, Wesley. The princess faults this pirate for the loss of her love, and screams at him...

"You have caused me so much pain!"

He retorts...

"Life **is** pain, Highness. Anyone who says differently is selling something."

Leadership can often be painful friends, anyone saying different…

It is hard to be leader. If it was easy, everyone would be great at it. Leadership is a moving target, steeped in nuance and circumstance. People are difficult and variable and emotional and ever changing, so leadership is all those things as well.

Remember the foundations. Trust and Respect. Begin your efforts with those, and it will serve you well.

Consider your intended outcomes until it becomes like breathing—remembering that every interaction, action or behavior, no matter how brief, has an outcome … has a consequence.

Find gifts in others and leverage your own as well. Use your gifts to transcend whatever stutter you may have in your life or your leadership journey!

Lastly, remember that relationships are leadership gold. Start them. Nurture them. Feed and grow them. Make them rich with all the intentful actions and behaviors that we have shared and considered throughout this brief book.

Never stop learning. Never stop moving forward.

Cheers!

TESTIMONIALS

"The best of the best in leadership growth and development. An amazing leader. An inspirational mentor. One of the best people motivators and coaches I've ever met. Lou Roden brings out the most in everyone he works with, taking teams from ordinary to phenomenal. Truly one of a kind."

—Peter Mack, CEO and Founder of
Collective Hotels & Retreats

"Even after 30 years of working within the hospitality industry, having the privilege of attending extensive hours of training, I have yet to find anyone more inspiring and passionate than Louis."

—Daniel Aylmer, Managing Director & Senior Vice President,
Greater China, Intercontinental Hotels Group (IHG®)

"In a world that often makes one doubt themself, it's the known we turn to. Louis is such a professional—he will help you believe in all that is possible and is already inside you waiting to manifest to the world."

—Arjun Channa, General Manager,
JW Marriot Phuket Resort & Spa

A WORD FROM THE AUTHOR

Whether you finished this brief book in an afternoon or in smaller pieces, I truly hope that elements within assist with your own personal leadership growth!

If you'd like to find out more about what I do for leaders and their organizations, please reach out! From keynotes at a conference to full culture and leadership initiatives—we truly love what we do and do what we love!

However, if you simply wish to network and begin a relationship, my door is forever open! I am confident that when we are in the twilight of our lives, none of us will look back and say, "I wish I had fewer relationships and fewer friends." Let's grab a coffee or a drink, virtually or practically, and talk, discuss, and share! Drop an email to LSRoden@InspireLSC.com and we'll talk!

Leadership never turns off. It never gets parked. It isn't a hat you take off or a behavioral flex that you make. Like being a person in general, it is a world view, filled with rich and genuine behaviors that serve all of those around you—any age, any role, and any place.

It is my dream to not only cultivate the relationships between leaders and their teams, but also the relationship they have with themselves. I look forward to hearing from you!

ABOUT INSPIRE CONSULTING GROUP

Our Approach

We believe that when people partner together, they do it not simply because they need what you have. An organization's promise and commitment reside in its purpose and mission. We are committed to moving beyond traditional, transactional consulting. Instead, we focus on forming relationships with our clients that endure.

We leverage best practices that have been cultivated with the finest hospitality organizations around the world to deliver leadership and service culture development programs that have impact. We marry our proven content, formats and program flows with the specific needs, brand elements and differentiators that are important to your organization.

Our Purpose

ICG is committed to the principles of inspiration and the basic truth that sincere service and leadership reside in the heart; when this inspiration is married with impeccable execution, loyalty and success is driven across any enterprise.

Our Commitment

We will partner with you with a common understanding— that by developing positive culture and building world-class approaches and curriculum that helps transform the work environment, we help foster deep loyalty with customers/ guests and team members.

We will do this by crafting programs that are relevant, practical, easily understood, and rapidly deployable to the workplace and to every place.

ABOUT THE AUTHOR

 Louis Roden has over 25 years of international Organizational Development and Service Culture experience. His transformational roles include serving in leadership positions in hospitality, global transportation and logistics, finance technology, and other service industries.

In September of 2008, Louis founded Inspire Consulting Group, an international consultancy dedicated to practical, reality-based leadership development programs, brand development and communication strategies, and exemplary service culture curriculums.

Made in the USA
Columbia, SC
21 July 2024

3c20bdf1-a924-45d2-b1e3-0e9599524896R01